N°5
The
West Midlands

by John Whitehouse & Geoff Dowling

Silver Link Publishing Ltd

The Coach House, Garstang Road, St Michaels, Lancashire PR3 0TG

British railways past and present.
Vol. 5: The West Midlands
1. Railroads – Great Britain – History
I. Whitehouse, John   II. Dowling, Geoff
385'.0941   HE3018

ISBN 0-947971-18-1

WORCESTER: The 'Vinegar Branch' ran about ½-mile from Worcester locomotive yard to the works of Hill Evans & Company, whose traffic it carried from 1872 until 1964. It was renowned for two level crossings over busy roads, which were protected by lower quadrant GWR-type semaphore signals, operated from a ground frame. Although the signals are not shown in this late 1950s view the character of the branch is clearly conveyed as '1600' Class 0—6—0PT No. 1639 cautiously approaches one of the crossings, whilst returning from the works. No. 1639, one of a class of 70 engines designed by Hawksworth and introduced in 1949 for light branch and shunting duties, was withdrawn in November 1964 and subsequently scrapped in South Wales in April 1965. Although all trace of the railway has vanished, the right hand wall and rear factory building positively pinpoint the location. *John Dew/GD.*

2

CONTENTS

ACKNOWLEDGEMENTS

Our thanks, for assistance in the production of this book, are due to: BR Press Officer John Wilber, Shand Construction, the CEGB, Ironbridge Power Station, Barry Geens, George Stevens and Ned Williams. Also a special word of thanks to all the photographers who have willingly provided us with archival material and who are credited with their work throughout the book. Hugh McQuade, of the Severn Valley Railway's Carriage & Wagon Department, was very helpful in ensuring that we could produce the Bridgnorth 'present' picture and this assistance was much appreciated. Finally, thanks indeed to the many railmen of several generations, who have directly or indirectly assisted our cause.

FRONT COVER: A lingering memory of Birmingham Snow Hill were its two clocks, one on platform seven and the other outside the booking hall; they still figure prominently in conversation, whenever a 'Brummie' recalls the 'old' Snow Hill station. "Under the Clock" was a favourite meeting place! On April 12 1962, the clocks were showing 1.55pm, indicating a 'right time' arrival for the up 'Cambrian Coast Express' hauled by 'King' 4—6—0 No. 6021 *King Richard II*. Not only does this photograph clearly show the marvellous roof but it also conveys the impression of abundant space created by the two main island platforms. The new station of 1987 follows a similar layout, but without the through centre roads. It consists of two island platforms with public access from an enclosed entrance with wide staircases. The 'present' picture shows the new Snow Hill on October 6 1987, with a four-car DMU awaiting departure on an evening commuter duty. The station opened to public services on Monday October 5, following the official opening ceremony, conducted by BRB Chairman Sir Robert Reid, on Friday October 2. Bridge clearance work in the tunnel has also created the possibility of steam traction once again gracing Snow Hill. *Peter Shoesmith/JW.*

To Daphne and Jean

First published in the United Kingdom, November 1987.
Reprinted November 1988.

Typeset by Lloyd Williams, Southport, and printed in the UK by Netherwood Dalton & Co. Ltd., Huddersfield, Yorkshire.

TITLE PAGE: The changing railway at Old Hill, north-east of Stourbridge. Main picture: '5600' Class 0—6—2T No. 6683 pounds up the bank from Cradley Heath to Old Hill with the 1.43pm Stourbridge Junction — Hawthorns Halt football train, a regular working at the time for West Bromwich Albion supporters living in the Black Country. The elevated position which Old Hill enjoys is apparent from this photograph, taken on April 30 1960. The locomotive is crossing the junction with the Windmill End branch, whose tracks curve away to the right, leading to Old Hill's second station, at High Street. Today (inset) the whole scene is dominated by trees, which have enclosed the main line and obliterated the track bed from the branch, closed on June 15 1964. A Class 116 three-car DMU approaches Old Hill with a Stourbridge Junction — Birmingham New Street 'stopping' service of 1987. *John Dew/GD.*

REAR COVER: An unusual visitor to Kings Norton on April 12 1963 (upper) was LNER Class B1 4—6—0 No. 61153, which is probably working empty stock from the carriage sidings to New Street, prior to forming a train to East Anglia. Note the extensive station platforms and buildings which reflect the fact that Kings Norton was often used as an 'overspill' station for New Street, when services would start and terminate there to alleviate the congestion in the city centre. Today, Kings Norton is part of the Cross City Line, with a new booking hall at the Cotteridge end. There is no longer access to the station from the footbridge, whilst the station buildings, apart from one structure on the southern end of the down side, have been demolished. On April 29 1987, Class 50 No. 50007 **Sir Edward Elgar** heads for New Street with the 7.30 Penzance — Aberdeen service. The left hand tracks lead to the Camp Hill line, the two lines being connected by a curve at nearby Lifford. *Peter Shoesmith/JW.*

INTRODUCTION

It seemed to be a relatively straightforward idea; collect a few old photographs, divide them between us and go along and photograph the location today. Simple? Certainly not! Collecting the old photographs was not too much of a problem, if a little slower than we thought, but when it came to taking the 'present' pictures, life was occasionally difficult, and sometimes downright impossible! For example, trees were a major problem, and it occurred to us that when the original photographer visited the scene he had dropped a sycamore seed which in the last 20 years has grown into a large, healthy tree! The exact angle for the shot would frequently not only be just behind the largest tree, but also obscured by a forest of saplings, growing from seeds from the parent tree.

Questioned by the police? Yes, that happened too. Whilst balanced precariously on top of folding stepladders in the middle of a traffic island now occupying the site of Donnington station, a 'Panda' car arrived. "Mind telling me what you are doing sir? . . .

"Photographing the railway station . . ."

"Oh yes." It's surprising how much disbelief a police officer can convey in two words.

After producing the old photographs and a lengthy explanation we managed to convince him that we were not press photographers photographing the strikers picket line at a nearby factory, nor were we spying on the adjacent Ministry of Defence Depot!

Quite a number of our old photographs proved impossible to duplicate, such as where former railway land had been sold and redeveloped in a way that would have made re-photographing the scene a matter of standing on someone's lounge, or where British Rail had electrified the line and it would have been too dangerous (and illegal) to even try. All was not gloom, however, for when a difficult site was finally pinpointed, often by an otherwise unimportant piece of fencing or a distant church spire, a real sense of achievement was experienced.

We also met some very pleasant people during our often unreasonable requests for access to their property; our special thanks to the lady now living at the former Hunnington station, who allowed a rather dishevelled motor-cyclist to prowl around her lawn, looking for a platform edge. On the other hand, the Mexican Eagle Owl whose cage is now situated on the platform of one old station we visited seemed much less friendly, his unblinking gaze appeared to be assessing our potential as a meal, if only he could have escaped from his cage! Fortunately, his owner was much more friendly.

Many scenes in this book highlight examples of railway cutbacks and closures, but there are also positive developments to report, for some railways in the West Midlands are experiencing a much-needed boost in the late 1980s. Snow Hill station, in Birmingham, has been re-opened from the south, and hopefully the track along the old Great Western route north from Snow Hill, through Hockley to Galton Junction, will also be reinstated to form a second cross-city line from Solihull to Stourbridge. At the time of going to press, proposals were also in hand to involve private capital in a Rapid Transit System which will hopefully utilise some disused railways.

Elsewhere, a more positive attitude towards railways has brought success; the Cotswold Line, only recently the subject of closure speculation is now buoyant thanks to an aggressive marketing and operating policy, whilst at Kidderminster, BR has acknowledged that steam is profitable by offering through tickets to the Severn Valley Railway. There is talk of further electrification in the West Midlands, possibly of the Cross City Line, but to date such thoughts remain as pure speculation, as the long-term local traction policy has still to be decided.

In the meantime, we hope that the contents of this book will stir some pleasant memories, and encourage deeper concern for our surviving railways. It would be impossible to cover the whole area in detail with such a relatively small number of pictures, but we have tried to achieve a balanced cross-section and we hope readers will enjoy our efforts. Finally, all the 'new' views have been taken especially for this book and whilst in a few cases it was impossible to stand in precisely the same location as the earlier photographers, 'by gum' we tried!

John Whitehouse & Geoff Dowling
Birmingham,
October 1987.

OPPOSITE PAGE: OLD HILL station, on the Stourbridge — Birmingham New St. line was an important junction; at the west end of the platforms was the Windmill End branch junction (see title page) whilst at the eastern end was the Halesowen branch junction. The station was on a gradient (leading to Old Hill Tunnel) and eastbound trains always faced a stiff climb through the station — until 1986, a banking locomotive was stationed at Stourbridge, to assist trains as required.

Top: In 1964, Old Hill station looked rather dilapidated as '6400' Class 0—6—0PT No. 6434 prepared to work an evening train to Dudley, via the Windmill End branch. The Halesowen branch (which had its own platform) can be seen trailing away to the right beneath the water tower. The tunnel is situated below the clearing on the ridge, above the locomotive. A rather unkempt modern brick halt greets the Old Hill traveller today,   as shown on July 8 1987, as Class 150 'Sprinter' DMU No. 150105 departs with the 1745 Kidderminster — Birmingham New Street service. The rear destination blind is a little misleading! *John Dew/GD.*

CENTRAL BIRMINGHAM

STECHFORD: On September 6 1958 (above) a three-car Metro-Cammell DMU calls at Stechford with the 4.10pm Rugby (Midland) — Birmingham New Street train. At that time the booking office was situated at road level on the overbridge, and the up and down main lines through the centre were flanked by relief lines. Just behind the camera is the junction with the line to Aston which allows traffic (particularly freight) to avoid New Street station. *Michael Mensing.*

Below: Today, the trees on the right grow on the trackbed of Stechford's former down relief line, and the station offers only basic shelter, as the booking office has been moved from the main road bridge and onto the side road, on the right of the station. In sunny weather on May 2 1987, Class 312 EMU No. 312201 calls with a Coventry — Birmingham New Street 'stopping' service. The gabled property on the extreme right hand side provides an element of continuity between the two scenes. *JW.*

NEW STREET: The London & Birmingham Railway reached Birmingham in 1838, and constructed a magnificent but inadequate terminus at Curzon Street. Realising the mistake, authority was obtained in 1846 for a new station to be built at New Street (originally known as Grand Central) which required extending the line by nearly one mile and included a tunnel and some stiff gradients. Officially opened in 1854, the station was used jointly by the newly constituted London & North Western Railway and the Midland Railway, which opened its own platforms in 1885. The station had two impressive train sheds, both with an overall roof. Wartime bombing destroyed the LNWR side, but the Midland roof remained until latter-day rebuilding. A new station was required for the electrification scheme and a consortium, which included private developers, rebuilt both New Street station and the surrounding central area. For those familiar with New Street today, this picture could be a revelation, as it shows a 'cut-away' version of the station as seen on September 29 1965, during reconstruction. Work is advancing on the Midland side, but the LNWR part is still in its post-war condition. Note the truncated remains of the famous footbridge, serving platforms 1-3. In the background is the familiar Birmingham skyline with the 'Rotunda and Bull Ring Shopping Centre. The trains continued to run throughout the reconstructions. BR.

NEW STREET: This was the view (above) on June 17 1987 looking east from New Street toward Proof House Junction as Class 81 No. 81011 leaves with a pair of Mk 1 coaches. The distinctive 'Rotunda' building stands above. *Michael Mensing.*

Right: It was a very different scene at this location on September 19 1959, as 'Patriot' 4—6—0 No. 45548 *Lytham St. Annes* waited at Platform 3 with the 12.15pm from Blackpool. The rear view of the Odeon (upper left) remains unchanged, but the warehouses above the tunnel were demolished to make way for the Smallbrook Ringway inner city ring road. *JW.*

NEW STREET: The overall roof on the Midland side of the station (above) was a distinctive feature until the time of reconstruction, and on February 1 1964 there is evidence of preparatory work for the rebuilding, as 'Peak' Class diesel electric No. D19 departs from Platform 10 with the down 'Devonian'. Note the lower quadrant semaphore signals just beneath the roof. *Michael Mensing.*

Left: Today's skyline at New Street presents a very different picture, yet two buildings are common to both photographs: in the centre is the Albany Hotel, whilst on the far right can be seen part of the Futurist Cinema building. On June 17 1987 DMU car No. 53885 leads a Longbridge-bound local service from Platform 9, whilst in the bay on Platform 12 stands the Class 08 station pilot. *JW.*

NEW STREET: A good impression of how this famous station has been enclosed is given by these views, from the eastern end of the present Platform 6. Above: In June 1987, Class 87 No. 87005 *City of London* (left) has just arrived from Glasgow, whilst a Class 86/2 has charge of a Euston — Wolverhampton service. Behind and above is a two storey car park which is part of the shopping centre. Another multi-storey car park stands on top of that, whilst the site of the Queens Hotel is now occupied by an office block. In the 'past' view (below) a four-car DMU leaves on April 16 1960, as the 4.55pm departure to Stoke on Trent. *Michael Mensing/JW.*

MONUMENT LANE: Stanier 'Black Five' 4—6—0 No. 44764 (above) lifts a heavy north bound express away from Birmingham New Street, and approaches the site of Monument Lane station on April 13 1964. By this time, the station had been closed for six years. The train had already passed Monument Lane engine shed, at the mouth of the tunnel leading to New Street station, and is now passing the extensive goods yard. *Peter Shoesmith.*

Left: This location has changed completely, with a housing development now occupying the site of the goods yard whilst the left-hand buildings have made way for a park and playground. A Class 116 DMU is passing with the 1830 Birmingham New Street — Great Malvern service on May 6 1987. The city skyline has changed dramatically, with few old buildings remaining in situ, such as the tower visible above the right-hand corner of the goods shed in the 'past' view. *JW.*

THE HARBORNE BRANCH had intermediate stations at Icknield Port Road, Rotton Park Road (the only crossing place on the branch) and Hagley Road, the latter situated on a main arterial road running west from the city. Pictured just before the First World War, Hagley Road station has an air of calm and tranquillity as the passengers await their train. Note the lady in the long dress with a parasol to protect her from the sunshine. The notice board to her right proclaims "London and North Western Railway" whilst many of the enamel advertisements carry names still familiar today. In those days the station had goods facilities and the yard seems well filled. *J.L. Marks Collection.*

Right: Today a walkway follows the course of the railway (closed to passengers on November 26 1934) but few remains of the station can be found. The terraced houses in the centre background have survived. *GD.*

HARBORNE: The Harborne railway was a commuter route through the popular western suburbs of Birmingham. Opened in 1874, it enjoyed in its heyday an intensive passenger service: Bradshaws of 1922 reveals no less than twenty departures daily from Harborne, of which five were between 7.26am and 8.49am. A corresponding number of trains left Birmingham New Street, with the busiest period, between 4.50pm and 6.00pm accounting for four departures. Freight also worked the branch, mainly to the Chad Valley toy factory and Mitchells & Butlers brewery. After a very profitable beginning, the branch suffered from increasing bus and tram competition and lost its passenger service in 1934. Also, from New Street to its junction at Monument Lane, Harborne services had to be interwoven with main line trains, which were always given precedence. Consequently, timekeeping on the branch was frequently erratic. However, freight continued until 1963. Two days before complete closure, the SLS ran an enthusiasts' special over the full 2½ miles of the branch, worked by Ivatt Class 2 2—6—0s. Above: No. 46522 prepares to haul the special away from Harborne station, witnessed by groups of local residents. Today (left) flats occupy the station site which can only be precisely located by reference to the long-gabled roof seen above the loading gauge in 1963.
Peter Shoesmith/GD.

ASTON: Situated within the junction, where the Stechford cut-off left the Grand Junction line to Duddeston and Birmingham, was Aston engine shed. On June 22 1957 (above) MR Class 2P No. 40356 approaches Aston (passing the shed on the left) with a local service. The train is leaving a section of quadrupled track, and the slow line can be seen diverging beneath the rear bogie of the last carriage. Four-track capacity was necessary, as until recently the (now closed) Carriage Storage Depot at Duddeston accounted for many trains, with attendant shunting movements. The wagon repair facilities, also at Duddeston remain at work today and generate traffic along that section. Today's scene at Aston (right) shows many changes; the shed has long gone and the site is now occupied by a motor vehicle distributor, whilst the high ground on the right is now an industrial estate. On June 13 1987 Class 304 EMU No. 304016 passes with a Birmingham New Street — Walsall service. *Peter Shoesmith/ Robin Banks.*

PERRY BARR: Nearly thirty years separate these views of Perry Barr, a suburban station on the Grand Junction route from Birmingham to Bescot, via Aston. On June 26 1957 (below) Stanier Class 8F 2—8—0 No. 48175 slows for signals with a down freight. The station is notable for its gas lighting, and the background is dominated by traditional terraced housing. A complete change has since taken place: the line was electrified as part of the West Midlands scheme and the modernised booking office is now situated at street level, whilst the terraced houses have been replaced by a modern office block. Left: Class 304 EMU No. 304016 pauses with a Walsall — Birmingham New Street service on March 1 1986. *Michael Mensing/JW.*

ERDINGTON: Located north east of New Street, on the line to Lichfield, Erdington is pictured (below) in the years before the First World War. On the up platform are signs advising passengers of the 'stopping' places of third, first and second class accommodation, whilst the notice board behind the 'Liptons Tea' enamel sign promotes LNWR Cambrian line services. On the down side, a member of the station staff is crossing the track after dealing with the recent departure to Sutton Coldfield and beyond. Note the tall signal post. *J.L. Marks Collection.*

Right: Today, one original building remains, which now accommodates the booking office on the up side. It remains in good condition and acts as a pleasing reminder of the past. On a July evening in 1987, a Class 117 four-car DMU departs with a Birmingham New Street — Blake Street service. Compared with the earlier view, the present day lack of advertisements is quite remarkable. *JW.*

RAILWAY STATION ERDINGTON

BOURNVILLE: For most of its length, the Birmingham West Suburban Railway runs along side the Birmingham & Worcester Canal, a glimpse of which can be seen in the 'past' picture (above) to the right of Bournville signal box. The photographer was standing with his back to the engine shed, and the water tower can be seen on the right, as a Gloucester RC&W two-car DMU passes with a local service. *Peter Shoesmith.*

Below: The same viewpoint on August 14 1987. The site of the engine shed is covered in rubble as Class 50 No. 50013 *Agincourt* approaches with an express from Penzance to Glasgow. One thing which has not changed is the quality of the dark chocolate, manufactured by Cadbury's at their Bournville Factory, which gave its name to the suburb, built by Cadbury's to house company workers. *GD.*

SELLY OAK: The Birmingham West Suburban Railway was conceived as a branch line, but its potential was realised by the Midland Railway, which extended it into New Street Station at one end and created a loop by connecting with the Camp Hill line at Lifford at the southern end. It thus became the main line into Birmingham New Street, a status it retains today in addition to its role as part of the Cross City Line, which now frequently creates problems when IC125 NE — SW services get 'caught' behind all-stations local trains. The latter-day development of the Cross City Line brought investment in new buildings to several stations, Selly Oak being one example. On April 15 1963 (above) Class 5 4—6—0 No. 45269 heads south at Selly Oak with an express duty, since when the passenger subway has been replaced by a new footbridge, located just behind the photographer. On August 14 1987 Class 47 No. 47547 approaches with a southbound service. *Peter Shoesmith/GD.*

KINGS HEATH: The 'Camp Hill line' from St. Andrews Junction to Kings Norton is nowadays regarded primarily as a freight route, although some passenger trains use the line, particularly on summer Saturdays, as it provides an effective by-pass for New Street station. When opened in 1840, it was the main line into Birmingham from Bristol, a situation which lasted until 1885 when expresses were switched to the Birmingham West Suburban line, via Selly Oak. A passenger service survived until suspension in 1941 as a wartime measure. It did not restart after the war, and closure was confirmed in 1946. Kings Heath station (below) was still almost intact, but decaying, in 1962 as a 'Peak' diesel electric passes with the northbound 'Devonian' on September 1. *Peter Shoesmith.*

Left: The station site was cleared in the late 1970s for redevelopment as a Furniture Warehouse and DIY/ Garden Centre. Behind the mesh fence, Class 45/1 No. 45106 runs light engine to Saltley in August 1987. Nothing remains of the station. *JW.*

BRICKYARD CROSSING: A pair of young trainspotters watch as Stanier 'Black 5' 4—6—0 No. 44659 (above) approaches Brickyard Crossing signal box with a northbound passenger train, probably a holiday relief, on September 8 1962. It has just passed St. Andrews Junction, having avoided New Street station, and will proceed directly to the Derby line at Saltley. *Peter Shoesmith.*

Below: The signal box has been the victim of modernisation, as the June 4 1987 view clearly shows, though the wall used by the train spotters still stands. Class 47 No. 47663 is heading for Saltley with a private charter train. On the right DMU is working ECS from New Street to Tyseley. There is quite a severe gradient at this point, which usually entails the heavier freight trains taking banking assistance from Saltley to Bordesley Junction, situated at the top of the incline. *JW.*

BORDESLEY: The Brunel route of the Great Western Railway finally reached Birmingham Snow Hill in 1852. Bordesley station, completed in 1855, was the first of three suburban stations built on the line, the others being Small Heath and Tyseley. Bordesley had quite extensive cattle docks, sited so that cattle could be driven directly down to road level and on through the streets to the nearby markets. The passenger station was busiest on a Saturday afternoon when many hundreds of football fans arrived for the nearby Birmingham City FC ground at St. Andrews. The circa 1964 view (above) shows 'Hall' 4—6—0 No. 5933 *Kingsway Hall* working a local service, probably to Moor Street Station. Beyond the station can be seen the fly-over for the Midland's 'Camp Hill' line to Kings Norton. *Peter Shoesmith.*

Above: The station at Bordesley has survived, albeit reduced to a graffiti-daubed, single platform unstaffed halt. The GWR buildings have given way to a vandal-proof concrete shelter and matching stairwell cover. On June 4 1987, a Class 117 DMU, car no. 51384 leading, works through the station with a service from Shirley to Birmingham Moor Street. *GD.*

BIRMINGHAM MOOR STREET was a terminus, dealing mainly with traffic from the North Warwickshire line. Built alongside the southern portal of Snow Hill Tunnel, its function was to relieve congestion at Snow Hill, which it outlived, due to its suburban role. When plans to re-open the line to Snow Hill were drawn, they included a new through station at Moor Street to be situated adjacent to the old station, at the mouth of the tunnel, with the old station scheduled for closure. Local pressure has, happily, ensured that the stylish old station will survive, possibly even as a terminus for a steam service from Birmingham Railway Museum at Tyseley.

Above: On April 23 1959, 'King' Class 4—6—0 6019 *King Henry V* heads the up 'Inter-City' out of Snow Hill Tunnel, passing Moor Street station, on the left. The bridge girders under the third coach carry the GWR line over the LMS line from New Street. Note the housing for the wagon hoist on the left. After closure of Snow Hill station in 1968, this trackbed lay derelict until work commenced for reopening, including the new Moor Street platform, opened on September 28 1987. On the opening day, a Class 116 3-car DMU is pictured (top) at Platform 2, ready to depart at 1240 to Shirley. The main body of the new station is to the left of Platform 1. Note the gradient dipping into the tunnel, defined by the tunnel lighting. The dip is deceptive, however, as a stiff climb to Snow Hill follows. *Michael Mensing/JW.*

SNOW HILL: Opened in 1852, Birmingham Snow Hill station has been rebuilt on three occasions; firstly in 1871 when an overall arched roof was provided, then in 1910 in the style for which it became renowned as a GWR station, and finally in 1987 upon re-opening after a period of some 15 years closure. Located on a narrow site, the original main line island platforms were of great length, with bays at the northern end used mainly for local traffic to the Black Country. In addition to the platform roads, up and down through lines were also provided and were used by a considerable amount of freight. When the West Midlands electrification scheme concentrated services at New Street, Snow Hill was doomed, losing its through express workings in 1968, with total closure following upon cessation of the remaining local services to Wolverhampton Low Level and Langley Green, in 1972. Fortunately, the closure agreement stipulated that the trackbed should remain intact, and now, due to the enterprise of the local transport authority, a new station receives commuters from the south once again through the re-opened tunnel. Above: The north end of Snow Hill, circa 1960 as 'Hall' 4—6—0 No. 4933 *Himley Hall* passes with a parcels train. The multi-storey building under construction is Lloyd House, now the HQ of West Midlands Police. By March 1987 (left) the new station was well advanced and overlooked by Lloyd House, so named as it was originally built for the Stewarts & Lloyds Steel Company. *Michael Mensing/JW.*

SNOW HILL: The view looking north from Snow Hill towards Hockley (above) as GWR 'King' Class 4—6—0 No. 6027 *King Richard I* restarts a Paddington — Wolverhampton Low Level express. On the left is the old signal box, which was replaced as late as 1960 by a modern route-setting box on the down platform. In the background is a stabled DMU. Snow Hill was an ideal place for trains to start, as each exit was on a downward grade. *Michael Mensing.*

Above: The same viewpoint on March 18 1987. The location appears rather desolate, but at this time the new Snow Hill station was taking shape behind the photographer and the longer-term hope is that Snow Hill's northern route can also be reinstated, to create a second cross-city rail link from Stourbridge to Solihull. *GD.*

HOCKLEY: This was the first station on the GWR route north of Birmingham Snow Hill. Not only did it have comprehensive station facilities, but also an extensive goods yard. On the October 4 1958 (below) an 0—6—0PT is shunting part of the yard on the right whilst '4300' Class 2—6—0 No. 6313 speeds through with a relief Hastings to Birkenhead express. On the up road, 'WD' 2—8—0 No. 90212 draws up to adverse signals with a train of empty iron ore wagons. *Michael Mensing.*

Below: The same scene today is one of total desolation, and although all traces of track and buildings have gone, the platforms are still generally intact. In an unusual piece of official foresight, it was decreed that the route should remain intact after closure, in case the railway should ever need to be replaced. The area is now in dire need of an improved transport system and a proposed rapid transit light railway utilising part of this trackbed is being investigated. *GD.*

SOHO & WINSON GREEN was the second station north of Birmingham, from Snow Hill, and boasted four platforms covering both fast and slow lines. It was situated close to Winson Green prison. The GWR station survived until 1972, when the passenger service was finally withdrawn and the line closed. In this view, 'King' 4—6—0 No. 6016 *King Edward V* speeds past on November 25 1961, with the up 'Cambrian Coast Express'. *Michael Mensing.*

Right: A sad contrast on May 5 1987, with the up fast platform still infact, but overgrown, whilst the centre island platform has lost its facing, the bricks having been used during construction of the Severn Valley Railway new station at Kidderminster. The most distinctive feature of the scene remaining is the spire, not of a church, but of Benson Road School. *JW.*

THE WOLVERHAMPTON AREA

WOLVERHAMPTON was important before the arrival of the railway, with good road and canal connections. The Grand Junction Railway skirted the town in 1837, but it was left to the Shrewsbury & Birmingham Railway in 1849 and the Birmingham Wolverhampton & Stour Valley Railway in 1852 to reach Wolverhampton itself, during which time the two companies fought over running powers on the Stour Valley line. Eventually, these companies were absorbed by the GWR and LNWR respectively. The MR also gained access from the Walsall line in 1879 but was never a major force. The GWR and LNWR each left a large station.

High Level station (LNWR) was a gloomy place with an overall roof which offered some protection as the station was in an exposed position overlooking both the GWR's Low Level station and the eastern suburbs. The station is pictured (above) in the late 1950s, with a Park Royal two-car DMU stabled on the centre road at the north end. The station was completely rebuilt during electrification, and the same viewpoint on June 20 1987 shows Class 150 'Sprinter' DMU No. 150121 arriving at Platform 2, from Shrewsbury. *Mike Payne/JW.*

COSELEY (DEEPFIELDS) is the first station south of Wolverhampton High Level on the Stour Valley line, and is served today only by local trains. In September 1966 it looked rather shabby (above) as a Metro-Cammell DMU called with a Birmingham-bound service. One surprising feature is that the platform canopies appear to be intact despite the presence of electrification masts. Only the down platform building was destined to remain however whilst on the up side a 'bus shelter' has replaced the traditional station building. Despite rationalisation, the station conveys a neat appearance on May 4 1987 (below) as a Class 86/4 approaches with the 1133 Shrewsbury — Euston service. *Peter Shoesmith/JW.*

STAFFORD ROAD ENGINE SHED: Although dilapidated, Stafford Road Shed (below) is brimming with atmosphere on August 24 1963 as three 'Castle' 4—6—0s are prepared to work summer Saturday trains to the West of England. From left to right they are: Nos. 7001 *Sir James Milne,* 5026 *Criccieth Castle* and 7006 *Lydford Castle.* The shed was always an integral part of the locomotive works, built by the Shrewsbury & Birmingham Railway and later inherited by the GWR. Locomotive construction ceased in 1908, after which the works carried out locomotive repair work, until total closure in 1964. *Hugh Ballantyne*

Left: The shed site today, occupied by light industry, all trace of the motive power depot having disappeared. The 'Castles' all perished: No. 7001 was withdrawn in September 1963, No. 5026 in November 1964 and No. 7006 in December 1963. *JW.*

CANNOCK ROAD JUNCTION marked the convergence of the GWR main line from Oxley and a spur to the LNWR at Bushbury. It was also the former northern limit of Brunel's broad gauge. On May 9 1965 (above) Class 40 No. D288, with a Manchester — Birmingham express, has been diverted via Wolverhampton Low Level because of electrification work on the Stour Valley route. Behind the train can be seen the extensive carriage sidings. When the track from Low Level was lifted, following the transfer of Shrewsbury services to High Level in 1968, the junction survived, but only for access to a head-shunt to allow Ironbridge-bound MGR coal trains to reverse. However, this operation ceased in 1983 with the opening of Oxley East Chord, which enabled coal trains to run directly from Oxley to Bushbury. *Michael Mensing.*

Right: The site of Cannock Road Junction on April 16 1987, with the track lifted and the formation neatly landscaped. Visible in the centre background is Stafford Road viaduct, which carries the Stour Valley line, to Bushbury Junction. *JW.*

WOLVERHAMPTON LOW LEVEL was opened in 1854 and until the 1920s had an overall roof. It closed in 1972, along with the through route to Birmingham Snow Hill. Until 1981 it survived as a Parcels Concentration Depot before eventually passing into the ownership of Wolverhampton Borough Council in 1986. The station is to be restored to its 1930s condition as a Transport Heritage centre.

Above: Contrasting scenes at the north end of Wolverhampton Low Level; on June 11 1962 'Castle' 4—6—0 No. 5031 *Totnes Castle* approaches the station with the 8.50am Birkenhead — Paddington express, which will probably be strengthened by additional coaches before continuing its journey behind one of Collett's 'King' 4—6—0s, which were officially banned from working north of Wolverhampton. Note the overall roof of High Level station on the far right. The scene today (Left) reveals that the trackbed now hosts a vehicle scrap yard. The skyline has not altered much, apart from the addition of electrification masts to the Stour Valley route south of High Level station. *Michael Mensing/ JW.*

MONMORE GREEN: From January 1 1963, all Western Region lines in the Birmingham area were transferred to the London Midland Region, whose influence can be clearly seen at Monmore Green on June 26 1966 (above) by the conversion of lower quadrant to upper quadrant signals. The train, hauled by Brush Type 4 No. D1697, is the 8.35am Birkenhead — Paddington service. By this time, all workings had been taken over by Brush diesel-electrics, because the 'Western' class diesel-hydraulics previously employed had a very poor reliability and performance record. On April 16 1987, a short stretch of truncated track remained, (left) merely as a headshunt for the nearby steel terminal. On the right, Monmore Green Greyhound and Speedway Stadium still dominates a now-barren railway landscape. *Michael Mensing/JW.*

PRIESTFIELD JUNCTION, situated nearly two miles from Wolverhampton Low Level, was the point where the Oxford Worcester & Wolverhampton Railway joined the direct route from Birmingham Snow Hill. In its heyday, it enjoyed the passage of the cream of GWR motive power. Whilst the layout of the station and junction is quite apparent, the scene (above) is one of terminal decline as a Class 122 single car diesel unit runs towards Snow Hill with the shuttle service from Wolverhampton Low Level. This service spanned the period between the loss of main line services in 1967 and total closure on March 6 1972. *Geoff Bannister.*

Above: Fifteen years later, in April 1987, the Priestfield platforms are still visible although a large pool now occupies the trackbed at the Wolverhampton end. Surprisingly, the Birmingham route is virtually clear of vegetation whilst the trackbed to Dudley (closed to passengers on July 30 1962) is now heavily overgrown. The days when 'King' 4—6—0s swept around the curve now seem sadly remote. *JW.*

BILSTON: Approaching Bilston on July 30 1961 (below) is 'Castle' 4—6—0 No. 7032 *Denbigh Castle,* heading the 1.10pm Paddington — Wolverhampton Low Level express. The industrial landscape was typical of the time, for the West Midlands was probably the most prosperous area outside London. All this was to change with the economic recession which brought many factory closures to the region by the early 1980s. No. 7032 was withdrawn in September 1964 and scrapped by February 1965. *Michael Mensing.*

Above: By 1987, the effects of decline are painfully apparent, for both factory and main line have gone. All that remains of the railway is a branch from Wednesbury, to serve the scrap yard on the right. Scrap trains run only as required, usually powered by a Class 08 0—6—0 shunter — a far cry indeed from the days when 'Kings' and 'Castles' graced the route. *JW.*

PRINCES END & COSELEY
was a Halt on the route from
Wolverhampton Low Level
to Dudley, closed in 1962. On
Sunday July 30 1961, Parcels
Unit No. 55993 restarts a
southbound pigeon special,
having just collected baskets
of birds. Although this Halt
had wooden platforms and
an ancient waiting room, the
station did have the benefit
of a concrete footbridge of
the latest pattern. *Michael
Mensing.*

Left: The same viewpoint on
April 26 1987, with the
houses in the background as
one of the few common
elements. The track bed and
cutting are overgrown, whilst
the bridge has been removed
and the cutting filled. The
branch should not be con-
fused with its LNWR neigh-
bour, which ran from Bloom-
field Junction on the Stour
Valley to Wednesbury line,
and survived until 1981. *JW.*

OXLEY JUNCTION: In June 1957 (above) GWR '2800' Class 2—8—0 No. 2850 trundles a Class K goods from Oxley Sidings to Baggeridge Junction, through Oxley Junction, towards the single line section through Tettenhall. The GWR provided a double track turn-out onto the Shrewsbury & Birmingham line, which was a measure of the activity at this location.
Geoff Bannister.

Right: Looking at Oxley Junction today, it is difficult to imagine the busy scene of yesteryear. Since closure in 1965 nature has made a vigorous reclamation of the railway, almost obscuring the houses on the left. This picture was taken in April 1987. *JW.*

TETTENHALL: It was not until 1925 that the GWR extended the old Oxford Worcester & Wolverhampton spur to Kingswinford northward to a junction near the present Oxley Carriage Sidings, thereby forming an effective avoiding line for Wolverhampton. Proposals for the construction of this line had long been mooted, and indeed, work had begun before the First World War, only to be delayed by a shortage of men and money. Although blessed with several stations along its route, the passenger service survived only until October 31 1932. Freight traffic continued until 1965. Although long closed, the station buildings at Tettenhall survived, albeit in a sorry state, as illustrated (above) on April 29 1957 as 'Hall' 4—6—0 No. 6944 *Fledborough Hall* passes at the head of a Crewe — Worcester freight. *Geoff Bannister.*

Above: In recent years, Wolverhampton Borough Council has renovated Tettenhall station building and goods shed as part of an urban walkway, and by April 1987 the scheme had been completed, forming a pleasing recreational area. *JW.*

SOUTH STAFFORDSHIRE

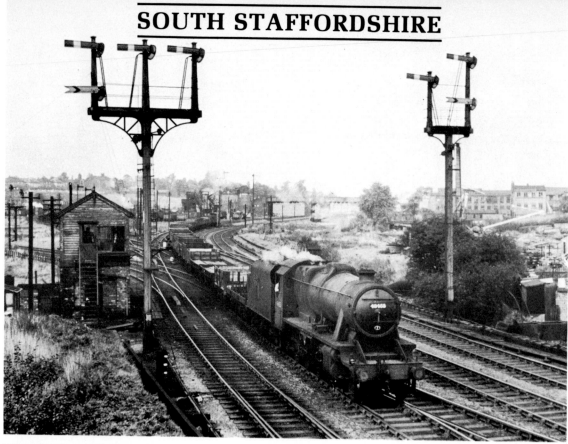

RYECROFT JUNCTION, one mile north of Walsall, once boasted four diverging routes as well as an engine shed. On September 5 1953 (above), as Stanier Class 8F 2—8—0 No. 48453 heads south with a freight, the routes are: behind the signal box (later to be replaced by a modern BR (LMR) design), the Midland route to Wolverhampton (via Wednesfield), and the LNWR line to Rugeley (via Cannock Chase). The engine shed was situated within the junction of the lines to Rugeley and Lichfield (via Brownhills), which curves away to the right, under Butts Bridge. On the right is the 'Sutton Park' line, from the Midland main line near Water Orton. The LNWR lower quadrant semaphores in the foreground were subsequently replaced by a single gantry. *Peter Shoesmith.*

Right: As pictured on April 16 1987, the junction has been heavily rationalised; the Wolverhampton and Lichfield lines have closed, and the shed site is now covered with trees. Class 50 No. 50036 *Victorious* is assisting rostered Class 47/3 No. 47357 with the Lawley Street — Holyhead Freightliner. *JW.*

PELSALL: The through route from Walsall to Lichfield closed in March 1983, although a short section from Lichfield to Anglesea Sidings, near Brownhills, remains to serve an oil storage depot. This once-busy line had gradually seen its traffic reduced until the remaining few trains could easily be diverted to other routes. The track has now been lifted south of Brownhills and the trackbed used in many places as a footpath, as at Pelsall station, formerly served by local trains from Wolverhampton, via Walsall to Lichfield and Burton upon Trent. Below: On December 2 1963 at Pelsall a Gloucester RC&W two-car DMU is working this local service, which lasted until 1965. After closure to passengers the station was soon demolished, and whilst the footbridge survived until complete closure, no traces remain today. *Peter Shoesmith/ JW.*

CANNOCK: The opening of the Cannock Chase Coalfield was significant to the development of the Walsall — Rugeley (Trent Valley) line. Initially opened as far as Cannock, it was later extended to join the Trent Valley, thereby creating for the future an important diversionary route. Freight, particularly coal and mineral traffic, have always been its mainstay, although passenger services survived until 1965. Above: On May 13 1963 a Park Royal four-car DMU arrives at the neat Cannock station with a Birmingham New Street — Rugeley train. *Peter Shoesmith.*

Above: On April 5 1987, a Class 47 is working hard to lift the Sundays-Only Newhaven — Manchester train up the gradient from Great Wyrley. Only part of the up platform survives. The line ceased to be used for diversions from April 1987; a sad event indeed, which will make local efforts to restore the passenger service that much more difficult. *JW.*

THE
BLACK COUNTRY

focus

SWAN VILLAGE: On June 5 1964, GWR 2—6—2T No. 4158 awaits departure from Swan Village, between Wednesbury and West Bromwich, with a train for Great Bridge and Dudley. The main line to Wolverhampton Low Level is behind the fencing on the left. The spur to Great Bridge (Horseley Fields Junction), although of only 1½ miles in length, was important to the GWR as it provided direct access to Dudley from Birmingham Snow Hill — a considerable commuter market. *Peter Shoesmith.*

Left: A return visit to Swan Village in 1987 revealed that the platforms have been obliterated to make way for a small industrial estate, although the distinctive road over-bridge is largely unchanged. The last passenger train ran to Dudley on June 15 1964 and the branch to Great Bridge closed completely on January 1 1968. *JW.*

WEST BROMWICH: To take the train from West Bromwich it is now necessary to use Sandwell & Dudley station, nearly two miles from the town centre. Thirty years ago, it would have been necessary to walk only 200 yards to the GWR station behind the High Street, which enjoyed a regular service, with through trains to Birkenhead and Paddington. On September 12 1958 (above) GWR 'Grange' 4—6—0 No. 6862 *Derwent Grange* calls with the 5.20pm Wolverhampton Low Level — Paddington express. The tall, shallow-roofed station buildings on the upside were typical of the line between Birmingham and Wolverhampton; regrettably they were demolished shortly after closure in 1972. As illustrated in the April 17 1987 view (below) the trackbed has been retained as a walkway and the landscaping has included both platforms, although the old up side has been shortened. Unfortunately the scene has been partially spoiled by graffiti. *Michael Mensing/ JW.*

KENRICK PARK: GWR '5700' Class 0—6—0PT No. 9753 (top) skirts Kenrick Park, West Bromwich, at the head of an up mixed freight on September 20 1958. A typical train of its day, but like the line on which it is travelling, a thing of the past today. as shown in the 'present' picture of this location, the course of the railway, closed on March 6 1972, is now utilised as a linear park and walkway. The surrounding scene shows only minor alterations, the most notable being the renewal of the road bridge to accommodate a dual carriageway. All may not be lost however, for long-term planning suggests a possible revival of the trackbed as part of a rapid transit system covering the Black Country area. *Michael Mensing/JW.*

OLDBURY was served for many years by local trains on the Stour Valley route between Birmingham and Wolverhampton, though it gained additional importance following the closure of West Bromwich in 1972. The September 1966 view (right) shows a Metro-Cammell DMU leaving Oldbury with a local service to Wolverhampton; the platform canopies have been cut back, electrification work is nearly complete and EMUs were soon to take over local workings. Although heavily affected by the recession, this area has remained economically important and in 1984, in order to tap the considerable longer-distance passenger potential, the station was renamed Sandwell & Dudley Parkway, served by main line trains as well as local services. Below: The new station on June 13 1987 as Class 312 EMU No. 312202 departs en route from Birmingham New Street to Stafford. This unit is one of four allocated to West Midland local services in addition to the more numerous Class 310s. However, plans are in hand to transfer the Class 312 units to the Great Eastern electrification scheme. *Peter Shoesmith/JW.*

DUDLEY: In happier days Dudley, in the heart of the Black Country, enjoyed an extensive local passenger service, encompassing Birmingham, Stourbridge, Wolverhampton and Walsall, and also Old Hill, via the Windmill End branch. On May 17 1963 (above) Ivatt Class 2MT 2—6—0 No. 46490 has charge of a parcels train, probably destined for Walsall. Sadly, all this disappeared with the Beeching cuts, the station closing on July 6 1964, but the line has remained open to freight.

The station site was redeveloped as a Freightliner terminal, with daily services to Nottingham and Glasgow; however, following rationalisation of the Freightliner network the terminal closed in September 1986. In April 1987 the loading cranes remained, rusting and unused, though ironically some container traffic has since returned, albeit as a storage facility for redundant containers awaiting sale. The church on the hill (centre) is a landmark for miles around. *Peter Shoesmith/JW.*

BLOWERS GREEN, about one mile south west of Dudley, marked the divergence of the Windmill End Branch (to Old Hill) from the West Midland Line to Stourbridge. On June 12 1964 (right) '6400' Class 0—6—0PT No. 6434 is propelling an auto-train onto the branch, adjacent to the extensive sidings which handled goods traffic from numerous local factories. Blowers Green station, behind the photographer, closed in 1962 with the withdrawal of passenger services to Stourbridge, although passenger trains to Old Hill continued to pass until 1964. The branch to Old Hill closed completely in 1968. *Peter Shoesmith.*

Above: The West Midland route remains open in the 1980s for freight traffic only, also serving Pensnett Trading Estate, but traffic may increase as a result of plans to redevelop the site of Round Oak Steelworks. Some through traffic remains, such as the 1402 Cliffe Vale — Exeter Riverside, which primarily returns empty china clay vehicles to the West Country from the Potteries. This train is pictured on July 6 1987, with Class 47 No. 47455 in charge. Of the branch, signal box and sidings, no trace remains. *GD.*

THE WINDMILL END BRANCH: was opened in 1878 and retained an intensive passenger service until 1964; in its latter days, whilst most trains were worked by GWR railcars, steam survived until the end on occasional trains and on May 29 1964 '6400' series 0—6—0PT No. 6434 calls at Darby End Halt with an Old Hill — Dudley train. The branch closed to passengers on June 15. *Peter Shoesmith.*

Above: A road deviation implemented since closure renders the site almost unrecognisable today, though some of the industrial buildings and the remains of the railway embankment help link the modern view with the earlier scene. *GD.*

THE WINDMILL END
BRANCH was known locally
as the 'Bumble Hole line', in
recognition of the Bumble
Hole area, situated close to
Windmill End Halt. Of the
remaining Halts, perhaps
Old Hill High Street served
the largest population. Its
short platforms and basic
shelter had been refurbished
just prior to this December
1962 photograph (above)
showing a Class 122 diesel
railcar approaching with a
Dudley-bound service. *Peter
Shoesmith.*

Right: It is not possible to
recreate precisely the 'past'
viewpoint today, as the
embankment and road
bridge have been removed,
whilst the station site itself
is now occupied by houses.
However, the location is still
recognisable by the row of
factory gables on the left.
GD.

STOURBRIDGE was an important industrial town, specialising in glass making prior to the arrival of railways, its transport needs satisfied until the mid-19th century by river and canal. The Oxford Worcester & Wolverhampton Railway put the town on the railway map in 1852, but perhaps of more importance was the construction of the route via Cradley Heath to Galton Junction — the so-called 'Stourbridge Extension', which gave access to the Stour Valley line and Birmingham's New Street Station. Additionally, a spur from Galton Junction to the Great Western at Handsworth enabled trains to reach Birmingham Snow Hill.

Above: Stourbridge Junction station comprised two island platforms, both with substantial canopies, and in this late 1950s view, a Fowler Class 4 2—6—4T No. 42418 stands in the carriage sidings with suburban stock. This side of the station has since been completely redeveloped; the carriage sidings have given way to a large commuters car park (below), whilst the fields beyond have been taken over by private housing. *John Dew/GD.*

Below, right: A 1956 scene, depicting GWR 'Hall' 4—6—0 No. 4961 *Pyrland Hall* at the north end of the station, with a mid-day Wolverhampton Low Level — Worcester train. A large goods yard, obscured by the train, closed in 1965 and the bracket signal has since disappeared, but in 1987 this viewpoint was otherwise little changed. The route still carries a busy commuter service provided by DMUs. *John Dew/GD.*

THE STOURBRIDGE EXTENSION

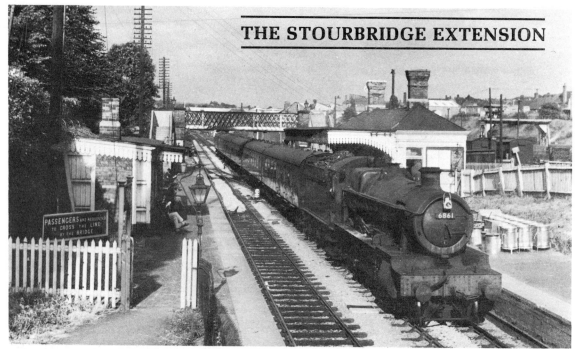

LYE was one of the 'Stourbridge Extension' stations which grew in importance in the 19th century with the development of local heavy industries. Behind the station can be seen the thriving goods yard which had the services of a modern travelling crane. Note also the locally-made shining galvanised dustbins on the platform, awaiting onward transit. The train is probably the 5.40pm Birmingham Snow Hill — Stourbridge Junction service, hauled by 'Grange' 4—6—0 No. 6861 *Crynant Grange*. The picture was taken during July 1964. *John Dew.*

Above: As shown in June 1987, the station buildings have been replaced by an austere timber booking office on the down platform and a 'bus shelter' on the up side. The goods yard is now occupied by a fuel depot. A three-car Class 116 DMU is forming an evening Birmingham New Street — Stourbridge Junction commuter train. *GD.*

Above: CRADLEY HEATH:
The large goods shed here was
a reflection of the considerable
industry the area once enjoyed,
and beneath the canopy are
the delivery vehicles which
were once a common sight on
West Midlands roads. A great
deal of traffic joined the main
line here from the Pensnett
Railway, a private system
owned by the Earl of Dudley.
In the foreground of this early
1950s view is GWR diesel railcar No. W22W, failed and
awaiting removal. *Ron Moss.*

Left: This scene has now
changed completely, the only
common point of reference
being the bus garage roof on
the right. The former goods
yard site was used by the local
passenger transport authority
for a road/rail interchange,
entailing a complete rebuild of
the station, which enjoys a
modern and attractive booking
office and waiting room. The
platforms are now conven-
tionally placed opposite each
other, after previously being
staggered, on each side of the
adjacent level crossing. The
new station and interchange
was opened in 1984. *GD.*

THE HALESOWEN BRANCH platforms at Old Hill in the late 1950s (below) as a goods train runs down from the main line. Headed by a GWR 0—6—0PT, the mixed freight is probably bound for Halesowen Canal Basin. Regular passenger trains over this branch ceased in 1927, although workers trains to the Austin Motor Car Works at Longbridge continued until 1958. Freight continued until 1969, when the lines from Old Hill to Halesowen and Halesowen Canal Basin closed. Palmers timber yard has since expanded to take over the entire site (lower) with the trees to the left screening the surviving main line. A pair of poles used to carry cables over the line (one of which is visible next to the derrick in the older view) are still in situ. *Ron Moss/GD.*

THE HALESOWEN BRANCH ran from Old Hill, on the Stourbridge Extension Line, to Halesowen Junction at Longbridge, on the Midland main line. Authorised in 1862, it did not open until 1883 and its passenger service was withdrawn in 1919. Strictly speaking, this branch was not part of the Stourbridge Extension, but geographically this is the logical point at which to illustrate Hunnington (this page) and Frogmill (overleaf).

HUNNINGTON was one of two intermediate stations between Longbridge and Halesowen, with a single platform and a substantial station house, now in private ownership. A goods yard at the western end served the neighbouring Bluebird toffee factory for many years. On November 2 1963 (above) a farewell rail tour is pictured at Hunnington, heading for Halesowen, behind Ivatt 2—6—0 No. 46522. Left: The station buildings, pictured here on April 5 1987, have been extended by the provision of a garage; note however the original platform edging between the two ladders on the lawn. *Peter Shoesmith/ GD.*

THE HALESOWEN BRANCH: A quite delightful scene at Frogmill Crossing on April 4 1958 (below) as '7400' Class 0—6—0PT No. 7448 approaches with a workmens train from the Austin Motor Car Works at Longbridge. The train has passed the distant signal for Halesowen Junction, where the branch joined the Midland main line, and is heading for Rubery, the next station on the line. Note the impressive crossing gates and the Midland Railway notice which belies the fact that the branch was jointly operated by the Midland and Great Western Railways prior to Grouping. In the distance can be seen the tall chimneys of the motor car works. *Peter Shoesmith.*

Above: The site of Frogmill Crossing on April 5 1987. The trackbed is now used as a private road to the car factory and No. 7448 is just a distant memory. *GD.*

MIDLAND ROUTES
NORTH OF BIRMINGHAM

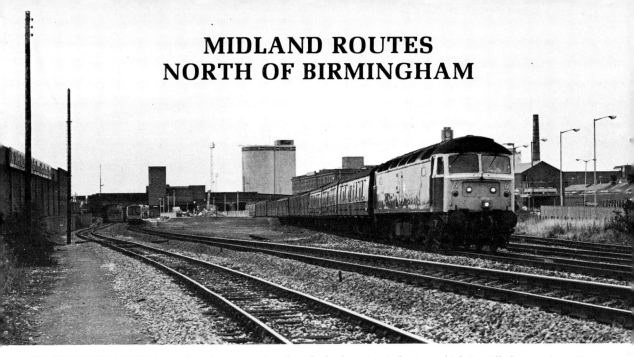

BURTON UPON TRENT has long been associated with the brewing industry, which is still the town's major employer. The giant Allied Brewery complex runs alongside the railway, the centre piece of which today is a massive silo, crowned by an electronic display alternately proclaiming the time or the temperature. Beneath is the station notable for its wide island platform. On August 5 1987 (above) the prototype Class 151 Metro-Cammell 'Sprinter' DMU is at the up platform with a Birmingham New Street — Nottingham service, whilst a Class 47 runs through non-stop with the 1243 Newcastle upon Tyne — Plymouth parcels train. *JW.*

Below: The same viewpoint on June 4 1963 as 'Jubilee' No. 45618 *New Hebrides* heads south with a fitted freight. The station had yet to be rebuilt and boasted impressive buildings and canopy, the platform then being longer to accommodate bay platforms. At this time, the private brewery railway system was extensive, with around 17 miles of track. Sadly, this has now disappeared and only a rationalised main line remains. *Hugh Ballantyne.*

STRETTON & CLAY MILLS station had been closed since January 1 1949 when Ivatt Class 2MT 2—6—2T No. 41227 passed through on June 4 1960 (above) propelling the 4.37pm departure from Tutbury to Burton upon Trent. The wood and tile buildings present a neat appearance and the platform nameboard is still in situ. The line was built by the North Staffordshire Railway and opened in 1848; passenger services were lost in 1960, and complete closure to Marston junction (on the Uttoxeter to Derby line) was in 1968. As pictured on June 7 1987, (right) the location has changed completely with all trace of the railway removed. The road bridge has been demolished and the cutting partially filled, with the course of the railway now defined only by the avenue of trees. *Michael Mensing/JW.*

FORGE MILLS station was situated between Water Orton and Whitacre, and this pre-First World War postcard (above) shows its impressive building and pleasant rural character. Soon after the Grouping of 1923 its name was changed to Coleshill, taking the name of the station on the Whitacre to Hampton in Arden line which had been closed in 1917. Forge Mills closed in 1968 and today the site is only located by the crossing, which retains its full-size road gates, although only a pedestrian wicket gate is in use. Adjoining the railway is a large complex owned by British Gas, once the site of the experimental Lurgi gas plant. *Collection of Dr. C. Hayfield/GD.*

WHITACRE was on the original course of the Midland main line from Derby, becoming a junction with the opening of the through route to Lawley Street in 1842, and later, the line to Nuneaton in 1864. It declined in importance after 1909, with the opening of the Kingsbury — Water Orton direct line, although freight continues to use the old route. Above In June 1959 a DMU approaches the station from the Nuneaton line, with the junction to Kingsbury diverging to the left. The station closed on March 4 1968. *Peter Shoesmith.*

Above: Whitacre station has been completely erased and the layout rationalised since closure, as shown in July 1987, as Class 31 No. 31427 approaches with a Yarmouth — Birmingham service. *Ivor Ford.*

STOCKINGFORD: The through route from Whitacre to Nuneaton, Hinkley and Leicester was completed in 1864 to provide an important connection between the West and East Midlands. Equally important for both passenger and goods traffic, it remains today part of an expanded cross-country route from Birmingham to East Anglia. Stockingford, an intermediate station west of Nuneaton, is pictured (above) on December 8 1962 as a Cravens three-car green-liveried DMU, complete with yellow 'Cats whiskers', pulls away with a Birmingham — Leicester train. *Peter Shoesmith.*

Left: Stockingford closed on March 4 1968, since when the platforms and buildings have been demolished, together with the chimneys on the skyline, as pictured on April 22 1987, as Class 150 Sprinter No. 150146 passes with a Leicester-bound train. *Ivor Ford.*

COLESHILL: When originally opened in 1836, the Birmingham & Derby Junction line ran from Derby, via Whitacre, to Hampton in Arden on the London & Birmingham Railway, in an attempt to win traffic from Euston, as well as Birmingham. This was not successful, and by 1842 a direct line to Birmingham Lawley Street from Whitacre had been built. A passenger service survived between Whitacre and Hampton in Arden until the First World War, and regular freight ceased in 1930. Later, the northern section became a crippled wagon store, whilst the southern section from Hampton in Arden was used during the Second World War for sand traffic. The track was lifted in 1952. The only intermediate station was at Coleshill (above) renamed Maxstoke on July 9 1923. It consisted of a single platform, with station house and waiting room. This photograph was taken from the road crossing and looks south-west. Closure came in 1917 with the withdrawal of the passenger service. In mid-1987 (below) some of the foundations of the platforms and buildings could be found amongst the bushes, but from the road there is no trace that a railway ever existed. *Collection of Dr. C. Hayfield/GD.*

THE TRENT VALLEY

STAFFORD: The opening of the Trent Valley Railway, connecting the London & Birmingham Railway at Rugby with the Grand Junction Railway at Stafford, was a major development. Not only did it provide a direct alternative route to the North West, but it relieved a potentially chaotic situation in Birmingham, which was already under pressure from rapidly expanding local and through traffic.

Stafford already had a station, one of the few provided by the Grand Junction Railway, but the arrival of the Trent Valley Railway considerably increased its importance. For many years Stafford was graced by an LNWR-style overall roof, which by 1961 had been partially demolished as part of the West Coast electrification scheme, as illustrated (top) on March 4 1961 as Stanier Class '5MT' 4—6—0 No. 44833 takes

the centre road with an up partially-fitted freight. The bases for the columns that once supported the overall roof can be seen between the down platform and through fast lines. Although the station was rebuilt in the 1960s, the track layout remained unaltered, as shown (above) on June 6 1987. Class 87 No. 87009 *City of Birmingham* is in charge of the 0956 Liverpool — Euston train. *Michael Mensing/JW.*

ATHERSTONE: These pictures provide an interesting insight into the changing character of the West Coast Main Line and its trains. Below: After spending many years under the threat of demolition, a partnership of private enterprise and local government has saved the attractive station building at Atherstone, on the WCML north of Nuneaton. It has now been renovated for use as office premises. Note too, the decorative lamp post on the up platform alongside Class 85 No. 85010, sweeping through with the Stirling — Kensington Olympia Motorail service, on June 10 1987. *JW*.

Below: The WCML at Atherstone in May 1961. Semaphore signals and ground 'dollies' complement the scene as 'Jubilee' 4—6—0 No. 45737 *Atlas* pauses with the 11.45am Liverpool — Rugby service. The lightweight train includes a pair of LMS-design coaches led by a BR Standard Mk. 1 vehicle. The splendid signal box straddling the up and down fast lines was lost during the electrification scheme; a new signal box was built at the Rugby end of the down platform. *Hugh Ballantyne.*

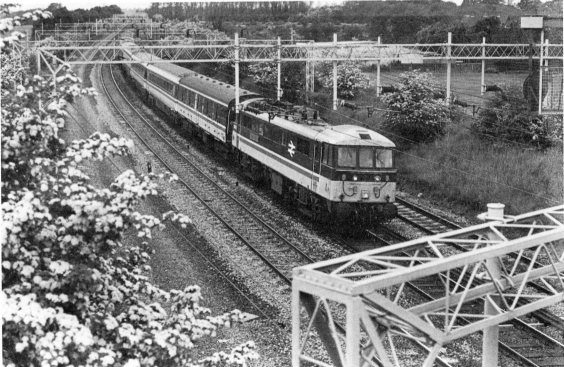

BRINKLOW: Although still a major trunk route, extensive rationalisation and modernisation have affected the Trent Valley line, which has lost much character. On Sunday June 26 1960, English Electric Type 4 (Class 40) No. D219 (top) leaves the southern end of Brinklow water troughs with the 12.35 Crewe — Euston service. Steam footplate crews kept a sharp lookout for the 'X' marker (illuminated at night) alongside the down fast line, for this was the point at which the tender 'scoop' would be quickly lowered, to pick-up water from the troughs. By May 30 1987 (above) the down slow line had been lifted; Class 86/2 No. 86231 *Starlight Express* is passing at the head of the 1030 Manchester Piccadilly — Euston service. The troughs are long gone, and note how the vegetation has grown in the intervening years; the houses to the right of the locomotive have been almost obscured by trees. *Michael Mensing/JW.*

RUGBY MIDLAND: In spite of the obtrusive catenary equipment, it is still possible to see that Rugby (Midland) station retains its general shape, although the goods yard to the right has completely vanished and the layout is much simpler than it was. In the background is the distinctive girder-work of the viaduct, now partially demolished, which carried the Great Central lines out of Rugby. However, the most striking contrast is the type of West Coast main line traction; On July 22 1961 (above) 'Princess Coronation' 4—6—2 No. 46225 *Duchess of Gloucester* heads the 1.30pm Euston — Perth, whilst 26 years later, on May 30 1987 (right) Class 86/2 No. 86214 *Sans Pareil* passes with a down express. This locomotive has been fitted with the jumper cables for the eventual push-pull operation planned for this route. *Duchess of Gloucester* was withdrawn in October 1964 and scrapped by the end of the year by the West of Scotland Shipbreaking Company, at Troon. *Michael Mensing/JW.*

RUGBY (GCR): The GCR came to Rugby in 1899, with its own station situated some way from the town centre. It was located in a typical GCR shallow cutting and had the characteristic wide island platform, as shown (below) on September 7 1958 as 'B1' 4—6—0 No. 61380 shunts empty stock for an excursion to Hull and Goole. The through passenger service from Sheffield to Marylebone was lost in 1966, the station surviving until May 5 1969, and the withdrawal of the paytrain service to Nottingham (Arkwright Street).

Above: Revisited on May 30 1987 the cutting, apart from a meandering path, is choked with trees and shrubs, though a closer inspection of the station area revealed that the platforms, part of the goods shed and yard still remained. The down line track bed is, however, now under water and forms a reed-edged lake. *Michael Mensing/GD.*

COVENTRY & DISTRICT

BIRMINGHAM INTERNATIONAL: On August 1 1963 (above) the most notable feature other than Class 40 No. D319 thundering past at the head of the 7.12am Leamington Spa (Avenue) — Birmingham New Street train, is Bickenhill Church spire seen to the right of the telegraph pole. Significant change at this very rural location followed Birmingham City Council's decision to build the National Exhibition Centre at this site; it opened in 1976. Birmingham International station was opened in the same year to serve the Exhibition Centre, and also the neighbouring, and expanding International Airport. A link between the station and airport was forged by 'MAGLEV' a revolutionary system whereby wheel-less cars, propelled by linear traction motors, are guided on an overhead track. This system can be seen to the right of the cab of Class 310 EMU No. 310080 (below) pulling away from International station, on June 17 1987 with a Coventry — Birmingham New Street local. Due to local road improvements British Rail has recently had to lease more land for car parking, to accommodate the growing number of passengers. The excellent service includes trains every half-hour to London throughout the day as well as connections to Gatwick Airport and the Channel Ports. *Michael Mensing/JW.*

FOLESHILL was the third station north of Coventry on the Nuneaton line, and for many years had a sizeable goods yard. Above on June 24 1961, Class 8F 2—8—0 No. 48686 runs tender-first from the yard with a northbound tank train. The prosperity of this line has always depended on freight traffic, and this applies equally today, with regular coal trains from the nearby Coventry Colliery. Passenger services ceased in 1965, but returned from May 1987, on an experimental basis, with a service from Stafford to Coventry, via the Trent Valley line. A two-car DMU rostered to this duty (left) runs past the site of Foleshill goods yard on May 16 1987. As this book went to press, it had been proposed that the Birmingham — Norwich service should be routed via Coventry, with the introduction of 'Super Sprinter' units, which if implemented would safeguard the future of the line. *Michael Mensing/GD.*

COVENTRY: The railway came to Coventry in 1838 with the opening of the London & Birmingham Railway and the city has since become an important staging-post. The facilities became increasingly cramped through the 1950s and with the implementation of the West Midlands electrification scheme it was decided in 1962 to rebuild the station. The old station is pictured (above) on June 27 1959, when 0—4—0 diesel hydraulic shunter No. D2910 was shunting vans at the west end goods station. Below: the scene has been transformed by the modern station complex, with longer platforms. A car park now occupies the site of the goods station and the road bridge has been rebuilt to accommodate both electrification and road widening. On May 30 1987 Class 86/1 No. 86101 *Sir William A. Stanier FRS* is leading the 1326 Wolverhampton — Euston service into Coventry's Platform 1. *Michael Mensing/GD.*

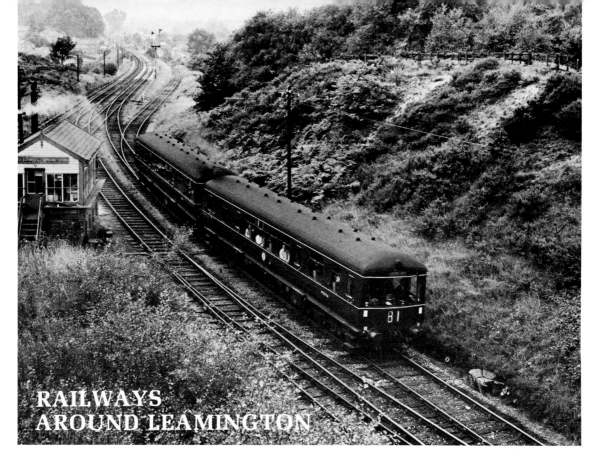

RAILWAYS AROUND LEAMINGTON

KENILWORTH JUNCTION was the point where the line to Berkswell diverged from the Coventry — Leamington route, and it enabled freight trains to either avoid Coventry and join the GWR line to Banbury, or rejoin LNWR metals beyond Leamington by travelling to Rugby or Weedon. Above: diverted from its normal route owing to engineering work on July 23 1961, a two car Gloucester RC&W DMU heads for Berkswell at Kenilworth Junction with the 9.30am Northampton (Castle) — Birmingham New Street service. *Michael Mensing.*

Left: The Kenilworth — Berkswell line was closed in 1965 and subsequently lifted, except for a short spur at Berkswell, occasionally used to stable the Royal Train. Reopening prospects were being discussed in 1987, as a result of a British Coal proposal to open a super-pit nearby, which would generate considerable rail traffic, but on June 11 1987 the site of the junction remains overgrown. Class 47/3 No. 47359 is leading a northbound inter-regional train past the site of the LNWR signalbox. *GD.*

MILVERTON: On August 30 1956 (above) Ivatt Class '2MT' 2—6—2T No. 41218 stands at Milverton at the head of the auto-train which ran from Leamington to Nuneaton, via Coventry. At the time of opening in 1844, Milverton was the southern terminus of the line from Coventry; extension into Leamington Spa was not authorised until two years later. The neatly-kept station was most attractive, its buildings being chiefly of wooden construction. *Peter Shoesmith.*

Above: Milverton station, closed on January 18 1965 when the Leamington Spa (Avenue) — Nuneaton (Trent Valley) line lost its passenger service, has been completely demolished and the site can only be identified today by reference to the road under-bridge, the girder work for which can be seen between the tracks behind the rear coach of the auto-train, and the current bridge railings alongside the fourth coach of Class 47 No. 47434, passing with the 0808 Manchester — Poole, in June 1987. *Ivor Ford.*

LEAMINGTON SPA: Until 1965, Leamington Spa had two stations: General, on the GWR London — Birmingham main line, and Avenue for LNWR trains from Coventry, Rugby and Weedon. They were built virtually 'back-to-back' and connected by a junction at the eastern end, shown here on October 7 1961, (above) as Stanier Class 8F 2—8—0 No. 48018 reverses out of Avenue Station, and onto the Great Western main line, with a raft of short-wheelbase wooden mineral wagons. When Avenue Station closed (in 1965) a new junction was provided at the western end to allow access from the General station to the Coventry line. On the right can be seen the distinctive girder bridge which remains a feature of Leamington Spa today as shown (left) with Class 31 No. 31143 taking the centre road, at the head of a northbound 'Speedlink' service, in June 1987. *Michael Mensing/GD.*

DUNCHURCH, one of three stations between Leamington Spa and Rugby, has lost one of its running lines since June 13 1959 (above) when Ivatt Class 2MT 2—6—2T No. 41227 called propelling the last scheduled train to stop at the station, the 4.30pm Leamington Spa — Rugby (Midland) service. The line closed to passenger trains two days later, but the link from Rugby was retained to maintain access to Southam Cement Works. Pictured (below) on May 16 1987, the station house is a private dwelling and the line is now disused. *Michael Mensing/GD.*

THE GWR MAIN LINE SOUTH OF BIRMINGHAM

ACOCKS GREEN: BR Standard Class 5 4—6—0 No. 73026 (above) trundles a heavy down iron ore freight through the relief road at Acocks Green on July 8 1959. The jets of water arching from the tender front indicate that the fireman is attempting to minimise coal dust on what appears to be a very hot day. The Acocks Green relief lines were installed between the wars to meet the demand for additional track capacity as freight traffic increased whilst the wide platforms were designed to accommodate substantial commuter traffic generated by Birmingham's southern suburbs. *Michael Mensing.*

Left: The much-rationalised viewpoint at Acocks Green on April 23 1987. The relief lines have given way to a commuters car park, which is unfortunately little used. A three-car DMU is approaching the platform en route to Birmingham Moor Street. The tree line bordering the railway has not altered much and the background is now clearer following the removal of the footbridge. *GD.*

SOLIHULL is a classic example of the decline of the railway in the West Midlands. In July 1961 (above) the Metro-Cammell 'Blue Pullman' is passing with the 4.50pm Paddington — Wolverhampton Low Level 'Birmingham Pullman' service. At this time, Solihull had an active goods yard and a substantial passenger station with both fast and slow lines, and a good service to Paddington and the South Coast. The 'Blue Pullman' trains, introduced in 1960, firstly for use on the Midland Main Line from St. Pancras, were finally withdrawn from Western Region service in 1973. *Michael Mensing.*

Above: Solihull presents a much-rationalised face to the world today, as illustrated on June 18 1987, as Class 37 No. 37250 approaches with the 1315 Didcot — Washwood Heath Speedlink coal train. Progressive decline here started with the LMR electrification scheme, which concentrated passenger traffic on the Euston line. Today, the only passenger trains calling are the well-patronised local services operating between Leamington Spa and Birmingham. The glass-faced office building occupying the former goods yard was used briefly by the British Leyland car company, whose short tenancy was followed by a period in which the empty building fell into disrepair. In late 1987, the building was being renovated in readiness for sale. The station has been reduced to a single island platform, the relief lines have gone and only a double track section remains. *GD.*

WIDNEY MANOR: A general view of Widney Manor station south of Solihull on the GWR main line from Snow Hill, on July 9 1959 (above) as 'King' Class 4—6—0 No. 6001 *King Edward VII* passes at the head of the 7.25am Wolverhampton Low Level — Paddington express. The substantial station buildings are well illustrated, as are the platforms on the relief lines, opened in 1934, when coincidentally, No. 6001 was one of four 'King' 4—6—0s used to conduct weight tests on the new bridge at the north end of the station. This must have been impressive indeed, as it involved all four locomotives, operating in tandem, running parallel over the bridge at speeds of up to 60mph. *Michael Mensing.*

Above: Widney Manor today offers only the most basic passenger accommodation. The relief lines were lifted when the former GWR main line route was downgraded at the time of the West Midlands electrification scheme, and part of the trackbed is now being turned into a commuters car park. The only locomotive-hauled trains to be seen in the late 1980s are freight services, the most common being MGR coal trains to Didcot power station, which is the destination of Class 58 No. 58009 seen here heading south on June 10 1987. *GD.*

LAPWORTH: On Sunday October 8 1961 (above) 'Castle' Class 4—6—0 No. 5031 *Totnes Castle* reverses from the up main line to the down main line of Lapworth, in charge of the 3.20pm Wolverhampton Low Level — Paddington, train. No. 5031 then worked forward 'wrong line' because of an engineering possession on the up line for permanent way work. Opposite the signal box is a small goods yard which mainly handled coal for a local merchant, although a large crane was provided, adjacent to the two box vans. *Michael Mensing.*

Right: On June 18 1987, Class 58 No. 58036 passes Lapworth at the head of a Didcot-bound MGR coal train. The up platform has been cut back so that only part of its original length can be used, whilst the goods yard site is now well-wooded scrubland. No trace remains of the signal box, and of the once extensive layout, only a crossover survives between the main lines. *GD.*

WARWICK: An evocative scene on May 8 1958 (below) as 'Hall' 4—6—0 No. 5991 *Gresham Hall* **passes through Warwick with a down iron ore train, and is about to tackle Hatton Bank. On the right is the coal concentration depot and the station is in the distance. Although an important historical town, Warwick never gained comparative importance in railway terms, always being overshadowed by its near-neighbour Leamington Spa.** *Michael Mensing.*

Above: An inevitable consequence of rationalisation at Warwick was the loss of the goods yard, now occupied by industrial units. Trains now have a 'clear run' at Hatton Bank, as the line is now a simple double track section, apart from the crossover near the station. On June 18 1987, a Class 116 three-car DMU runs towards Warwick, with a Birmingham Moor Street — Leamington Spa service. *GD.*

THE NORTH WARWICKSHIRE LINE

THE NORTH WARWICKSHIRE LINE: Birmingham and Stratford-upon-Avon were connected by the North Warwickshire line, completed by the GWR in 1901 from Tyseley to Bearley Junction. The GCR considered using the route as part of its proposed through line to London, but lost interest following intervention by the GWR, which was anxious to protect its own main line to Paddington from competition. The line did eventually become part of a through route, from Birmingham to Bristol, enabling the GWR to be independent of the MR. Later, it became a significant commuter route to Birmingham. BR attempted closure in 1971, but a court injunction prevented this, although at the time of going to press, the section from Henley in Arden to Bearley Junction has a closure notice posted.

TYSELEY: The North Warwickshire Railway diverged from the GWR main line at the south end of Tyseley, and is seen curving away on the right of the past picture (above) near the tower of the now-demolished Baptist Church. Running in from the left is the main line from Paddington (via Leamington), which on Sunday November 4 1962 was occupied by 'Western' No. 1007 *Western Talisman* with the 9.30am Paddington — Chester. The locomotive was one of the first of the 'Westerns' to be withdrawn, following the Ealing derailment of 1974. Right: A recently transferred ex-Marylebone four-car DMU approaches Tyseley station, behind the photographer, at the much-rationalised junction, on August 21 1987 1987. *Michael Mensing/GD.*

SPRING ROAD (above) was built in response to the outward spread of Birmingham's suburbs, and on the left are traditional semi-detached houses built in the inter-war years. However, Spring Road Platform, as it was described in the 1922 'Bradshaws', has a rather rural air as a six-car DMU pauses with the 11.36am Stratford upon Avon — Birmingham Moor Street on July 31 1961. *Michael Mensing.*

Above: The 1987 view of Spring Road was much more urban in character, as a result of the line now being straddled by a two-storey car park, built for the neighbouring Lucas Automotive Products Factory. However, the station still boasts a GWR type name board, adjacent to the Class 116 DMU calling en route to Birmingham Moor Street. *GD.*

36.

HENLEY IN ARDEN is the major station on the southern part of the North Warwickshire line, serving an attractive and popular town. It was once a junction, and in the earlier view (above) the line to Rowington (on the GWR main line) can be seen diverging to the right beyond the signal box. The Rowington line (opened in 1894) was not successful and closed to passengers in 1916 and to goods two years later. The branch line terminus station at Henley in Arden was retained for goods until 1962. The view in April 1987 looking north, shows that the signal box and GWR station name board have survived and even the steps to the long-departed shelter behind the name board are still buried in the undergrowth. A Class 116 three-car DMU is approaching with a Birmingham Moor Street — Stratford upon Avon service. If British Rail proposals, current as this book went to press, are implemented, Henley in Arden will become a terminus station, for the line to Bearley Junction is the subject of a closure plan. *Collection of J.L. Marks/GD.*

MIDLAND METALS SOUTH OF BIRMINGHAM

BROMSGROVE, looking south in the late 1960s, had an extensive track layout to accommodate both banking movements and goods traffic into the large yards. Two large signal gantries were necessary to control operations, as seen here from the platform end (above) as BR Standard Class 4MT 4—6—0 No. 75022 waits on the main line, probably for banking assistance, whilst a Stanier Class 5MT 4—6—0 takes water. An English-Electric Type 3 diesel electric locomotive shunts the up yard. *Ron Swift.*

Left: A similar viewpoint on July 6 1987, as an HST approaches at speed over the realigned main line which permits a faster approach to the 1 in 37 climb to Blackwell. On the left the former goods yard awaits redevelopment, whilst the up yard has been replaced by an oil storage depot. The stabling point for banking locomotives was to the rear of the HST, on the right. *GD.*

BROMSGROVE, at the foot of the Lickey Incline, has changed significantly since steam days. The 'past' picture (top) depicts Bromsgrove station in the 1950s, and clearly shows the change in gradient beyond the footbridge. On the right is the wagon works. Latter-day rationalisation has included the removal of the down platform and the realignment of the main lines enabling a higher line speed on the 1 in 37 gradient to Blackwell. The degree of change is clearly indicated by the course of the former platform edge, visible in the centre foreground. Today's local passenger services running between Birmingham and Worcester use the single, shortened up platform, down trains gaining access via the crossover visible in the modern view (above), beyond HST power car No. 43082, leading the 1125 Newcastle — Penzance service. Bromsgrove was listed for closure in the Beeching plan, but thanks largely to the efforts of the Bromsgrove Passenger Action Group, and limited support from the local authority, its future seems secure. *Ron Swift/Robin Banks.*

BARNT GREEN is the junction for the Redditch branch and also the boundary between BR's London Midland and Western Regions. Main line trains have long ceased to stop, but an hourly branch line service operates to Redditch as part of Birmingham's Cross City Link. Barnt Green once possessed extensive buildings, the station house, being situated within the junction whilst on the up platform the W.H. Smith kiosk and large waiting room indicated the large numbers of passengers who once used the station. Above: On July 31 1954 a trio of passengers wait on the down platform whilst 'Black 5' 4—6—0 No. 44810 drifts through at the head of a rake of 'blood and custard' liveried LMS coaches. *Peter Shoesmith.*

Above: By April 18 1987 the site of the up platform buildings could still be clearly identified as HST set No. 253004 speeds through with the 1109 Cardiff — Newcastle IC125 service. *GD.*

REDDITCH: The Birmingham — Gloucester loop line ran from Barnt Green to Ashchurch, via Redditch and Evesham. Owned by the Midland Railway, it was complementary to the main line (via the Lickey Incline) and provided access to the rich agricultural belt of north west Worcestershire. Passenger services were progressively withdrawn between 1963 and 1964 and all that remains today is the single line from Barnt Green to Redditch, now a booming 'new town'. On June 1 1963 (above) Ivatt Class 2MT 2—6—0 No. 46443 (now preserved on the Severn Valley Railway) stands in the old station at Redditch with a Birmingham — Evesham train. Following closure of the Redditch — Ashchurch section from June 17 1963, the old station site was vacated and the cutting filled. On the site today stands a bus stop and vehicle turning point, as illustrated on April 5 1987 and the new station is situated some way behind this location. Redditch is now at the southern end of Birmingham's Cross City Line and the rail service is subsidised by Hereford & Worcester County Council, from a point just beyond **Longbridge**. *Peter Shoesmith/GD.*

STUDLEY & ASTWOOD BANK was the first station south of Redditch, and possessed a station house, goods shed and distinctive Midland Railway signal box. Below: On April 4 1959, Stanier '8F' 2—8—0 No. 48700 passes in charge of a northbound freight. Note the lower quadrant signal. The station closed in 1962, one year before the end of passenger services, and freight ceased in 1964. *Peter Shoesmith.*

Above: In Spring 1987, the station and goods buildings remained in apparently good condition, both being occupied. The trackbed, however, has disappeared beneath a mat of scrub and grass; a sad sight indeed. *GD.*

BROOM JUNCTION was the point at which the Stratford upon Avon & Midland Junction Railway diverged from the Birmingham and Gloucester loop line. The island platform station survived until 1963, when passenger services from Evesham and Ashchurch were withdrawn. However, the last passenger trains called in 1962, for a replacement bus service had operated between Evesham and Redditch since October 1 that year, because of poor trackwork. The passenger service from Broom to Stratford upon Avon (Old Town) via SMJR metals had been axed by the LMS as early as 1947. On March 30 1959 (above) Birmingham — Ashchurch trains cross, both hauled by Ivatt Class 4MT 2—6—0s. Between the locomotives can be seen Broom Junction North Signalbox. *Peter Shoesmith.*

Above: The sad sight greeting latter-day visitors to Broom Junction. The road bridge has been demolished but the platform edging and some buildings survive as part of a Council Highways Department yard. *GD.*

STRATFORD UPON AVON OLD TOWN: The Stratford upon Avon & Midland Junction Railway was conceived as a freight route connecting Northamptonshire with Bristol, chiefly for the carriage of iron ore. A passenger service operated until 1952, but it was freight that kept the line going until closure in 1965. The SMJ station at Stratford upon Avon (Old Town) was a curious place, with an abandoned signal box (a remnant of the East and West Junction Railway) situated behind the operational signal box and an unusual platform canopy, both visible in the 'past' view (above). The train is a railtour run on May 24 1955 hauled by GWR '9000' Class 'Dukedog' 4—4—0 No. 9015. The tour ran via the SMJ route to Broom Junction; the tracks on the left led to the GWR exchange sidings. The engine shed can be seen on the right. *Hugh Ballantyne.*

Left: On July 11 1987, only the platform facings remained, although the gap for the point rodding from the old EWJR signal box is still discernible in front of the large bush on the left. *GD.*

THE COTSWOLD LINE

EVESHAM once boasted two stations, for the GWR and the MR stations shared opposite sides of a common forecourt. The GWR route to Worcester was part of the Oxford Worcester & Wolverhampton Railway, whilst the Midland line ran from Barnt Green to Ashchurch, via Redditch, on the Birmingham to Gloucester loop line, and crossed the GWR route east of the town, before turning south beyond the station. Above: On March 9 1958, a six-car 'Swindon' Inter City DMU runs into the GWR station with the 9.00am Swansea High Street — Birmingham Snow Hill service, having just crossed from the Midland route because of engineering work on the Stratford — Cheltenham line. An interesting bracket signal controls the down road whilst on the right stands an imposing goods shed. *Michael Mensing.*

Above: A visit to Evesham on April 19 1987 revealed that the goods facility, semaphore signals and water tower have now gone, as Class 50 No. 50010 *Monarch* awaited departure with the 1610 Paddington — Hereford. *JW.*

EVESHAM: 'The Railway Hotel' (centre background) enjoys a commanding view of the fluctuating fortunes of Evesham's two stations. The GWR station is on the left (see also page 88) but the Midland lines had long since gone by April 1987. The station building (closed in 1963) survives as a store. In the 'past' view on April 14 1962, Ivatt Class 4MT 2—6—0 No. 43046 shunts the stock of the recently arrived 1.06pm train from Birmingham New Street. Interesting details in the goods yard include the hand-crane, and also the delivery lorry, painted in early BR livery, together with the vans in the GW goods dock, served by the track running through the goods shed.
Michael Mensing/JW.

HONEYBOURNE, situated on the 'Cotswold Line' from Worcester to Oxford, Honeybourne was also important due to the nearby Cheltenham — Stratford upon Avon line, nearly one mile east of the station. Above: Honeybourne, just prior to closure on May 5 1969. This substantial station served a wide-spread rural community, who after considerable lobbying succeeded in having the station reopened in 1981. As illustrated on July 6 1987, the present buildings are very basic, consisting only of a 'Portacabin' and 'Portaloo'. A Class 101 DMU is approaching with the local all-stations service between Oxford and Worcester. Beyond the road bridge, which appears to have been considerably re-built, is the spur to the MOD Depot at Long Marston. *Ron Swift/GD.*

LONG MARSTON: With the opening of its Cheltenham — Stratford upon Avon line in 1908, the GWR achieved its ambition of owning an independent route from Bristol to Birmingham, albeit around ten miles longer than the competing Midland line, via the Lickey Incline. The GWR route passed through mainly rural areas and was well-endowed with stations, such as Long Marston, shown in our 'past' picture. Situated on the northern section between Honeybourne and Stratford upon Avon, the station enjoyed a service of nine up and eight down passenger trains daily. Long Marston closed to passengers on January 3 1966, and freight traffic on the line ceased in 1976. *J.L. Marks Collection.*

Above: In 1987, Long Marston was served only by a spur from Honeybourne to the MOD depot and Birds Scrapyard, but at the station itself the line has been lifted. Surprisingly, on March 29 1987 the platforms and signal box remained in situ. A plan by the Gloucestershire Warwickshire Railway to reopen part of this through route had by late 1987 resulted in the re-instatement of 2½ miles of track between Toddington and Winchcombe, on the southern section of the route. *GD.*

WORCESTER ENGINE SHED was host to rather grimy locomotives of GWR, LMS and BR Standard design when photographed on August 27 1961. Of interest is the variety of freight types, indicating the importance of the city as an industrial centre. Worcester's large goods shed and yard are on the left. The foreground repeating signal is on the spur from Tunnel Junction to Rainbow Hill Junction, which enabled trains to avoid Shrub Hill station and run directly to the Hereford line. *Michael Mensing.*

Right: The shed presented a very different picture in July 1987, for the foreground is now a vehicle park whilst the locomotive shed has lost its roof, thereby revealing a better view of Shrub Hill station. The once extensive goods yard has totally disappeared, together with the shed's large freight locomotive allocation. By late 1987, only a single Class 37 was required, for Worcester's final remaining freight working, the daily 'trip' to Long Marston MOD depot. The DMUs work local services to Birmingham, Oxford and Hereford. The repeating signal remains, but the line to Hereford is worked as a dual single line as far as Henwick Junction (on the outskirts of the city) thus abolishing Rainbow Hill Junction. Also, just in front of the Transit van, is the trackbed of the 'vinegar branch', (see page 2) dropping away to the right beneath the main line from Shrub Hill station. *GD.*

THE SEVERN VALLEY RAILWAY

KIDDERMINSTER: An extension line was built in 1878 to link Bewdley with Kidderminster, giving Severn Valley line trains access to the West Midlands. The station had a large goods warehouse and yard, seen beyond GWR 2—6—0 No. 6332 (above) heading south through the station with a mixed goods train on July 29 1960. *Brian Moone.*

Left: Following a successful share-issue, the SVR bought the Foley Park — Kidderminster link and by summer 1987 had built a new GWR-style terminus on the former goods yard. The new station is visible adjacent to 'Sprinter' No. 150146, operating a Birmingham — Cardiff service. The goods warehouse has also been bought by the SVR for use as a C&W Department headquarters. *JW.*

KIDDERMINSTER once enjoyed extensive freight facilities, as illustrated (above) on September 16 1961, as Class 9F 2—10—0 No. 92219 musters a train of short wheel-base vans, whilst a diesel shunter stands in the yard. The main line to Droitwich is on the left, whilst the Severn Valley line curves around to the right at the rear of the yard. The picture gives a clear indication of the intensity of West Midlands goods traffic in the closing years of steam traction. *Brian Moone.*

Above: Today, only part of the yard remains, used by the SVR for empty coaching stock. On May 24 1987, GWR 2—6—2T No. 4566 propels its train into the yard, after working in from Bridgnorth. Note the signal gantry, erected in anticipation of the commissioning of Kidderminster signalbox during late 1987. This gantry formerly stood on the West of England main line at Taunton. In the foreground is the connecting spur to the BR main line. *JW.*

ARLEY: It would be very easy to mistake the past and present views of this attractive little station, which although derelict in later BR days, is now in the care of the Severn Valley Railway. The SVR enjoys an enviable reputation for the quality of its restorations and this extends beyond locomotives and rolling stock to signalling and buildings, as illustrated by these views, separated by 16 years. In 1971 (below) BR had only recently abandoned the route south from Alveley Colliery, but eight years of neglect since the closure of the station is clearly evident. *P.J.G. Ransom.*

Below: By 1974 the SVR extended south and Arley was re-opened, with restoration in the hands of a particularly keen band of enthusiasts. A past winner of the Association of Railway Preservation Societies annual Best Restored Station award, Arley is frequently seen nowadays 'on screen' when TV or film scripts require a 'period' station scene. The loop has been reinstated and the provision of a signalbox has enabled the station to be used as a passing place by SVR trains. It is a marvellous place to spend a couple of hours sitting on a bench — after travelling on the train, of course. *JW.*

BRIDGNORTH: The Severn Valley line linked Hartlebury, via Stourport on Severn, with Bewdley, Bridgnorth Ironbridge and Shrewsbury. Opened in 1862, it was never particularly successful, and suffered from road competition in its latter years. The passenger service and through freight traffic were lost in 1963, although freight survived on the southern section, from Alveley Colliery, until 1970. In 1965, a group of enthusiasts decided to preserve part of the line and operate a steam service, which was inaugurated in 1970 between Bridgnorth and Hampton Loade. A share issue led to the extension to Bewdley in 1974, followed by another highly successful issue in 1984 which raised the £½ million needed to extend into Kidderminster and finance the building of a brand new station. In the late 1950s, Bridgnorth was a tranquil place, enjoying only a sparse passenger service interspersed by the occasional freight. The station supported a goods yard and had a useful hand-crane in the goods bay. In our past view, Fowler 2—6—4T No. 42420 stands at the platform with a Shrewsbury working in May 1957. *Geoff Bannister.*

Right: Bridgnorth today is a hive of activity, the goods yard now occupied by the engine shed and workshops. The track layout has been modified slightly but the bay platform survives for use by the Carriage & Wagon Department, although the crane has been removed. On August 15 1987, 0—6—0 diesel shunter No. 3566 has just cleared coaching stock from the bay and is reforming the rake to take account of restoration priorities. On the right stands preserved 'Western' Class 52 Diesel Hydraulic No. D1052. *Western Courier. JW.*

RAILS AROUND TELFORD

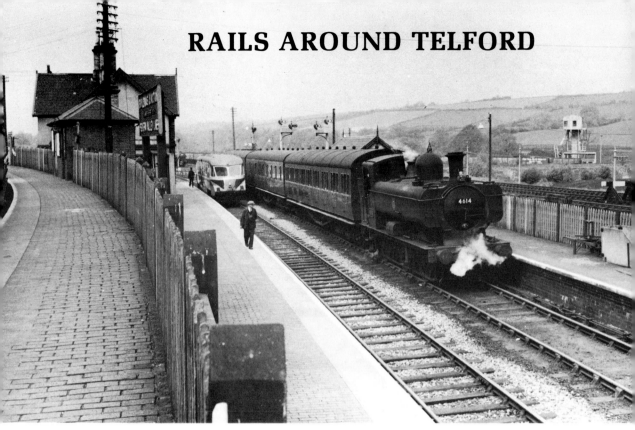

BUILDWAS JUNCTION was important, for it was possible to travel to Ludlow via Craven Arms; to Droitwich via Bewdley (the Severn Valley line; to Shrewsbury (either through Ketley Junction and Wellington or more directly through Sutton Bridge Junction) and to Wolverhampton, via Madeley Junction. The Craven Arms line platform diverged on a steep gradient, illustrated in the late 1950s view (above) as a train for Much Wenlock awaits departure from the higher platform. On the 'low level' platforms, Severn Valley line trains are crossing; the GWR railcar is heading for Shrewsbury, whilst 0—6—0PT No. 4614 is bound for Hartlebury and Worcester. Following the departure of these trains all activity ceased for hours, disturbed only by the passing of an occasional train for the nearby power station. *Geoff Bannister.*

Left: In the late 1960s, the old power station was replaced by a much larger coal-fired plant on the opposite side of the railway, and the site of Buildwas Junction station (closed in September 1963) is now occupied by the discharge plant for MGR coal trains. On April 14 1987, Class 58 No. 58044 draws a coal train from Baddesley Colliery through the discharge terminal, from which coal can either be fed directly to the burners or to storage hoppers. *GD (Courtesy of CEGB).*

COALBROOKDALE: GWR 0—6—0PT No. 3732 (above) calls at Coalbrookdale on May 5 1957 with the 12.48pm Ketley — Much Wenlock 'mixed' train. Following the withdrawal of the passenger service on July 23 1962, the line from Buildwas Junction to Ketley Junction closed, whilst the Coalbrookdale branch to Madeley Junction assumed increased importance by providing access to Ironbridge Power Station. *Geoff Bannister.*

Above: On April 14 1987 Class 20s Nos. 20032 and 20128 head a loaded MGR service through Coalbrookdale, which is pictured receiving a temporary platform, in anticipation of a sponsored summer service to the Ironbridge Gorge Museum. Coalbrookdale is the home of Abraham Darby's iron works and is considered to be the birthplace of the Industrial Revolution. *GD.*

MADELEY JUNCTION, south east of Telford, is the point where the Coalbrookdale branch joins the Shrewsbury — Wolverhampton main line. In December 1966 (above) Stanier '8F' 2—8—0 No. 48035 is surrounded by green fields, as it runs into the refuge siding at Madeley with empty coal wagons from Ironbridge Power Station. *Geoff Bannister.*

Above: The Telford area has seen considerable development in recent years as a result of its 'New Town' status, and the land around the junction is now fully occupied by industry. The railway has seen changes too, the signal box having been resited from alongside the up main line to within the junction and is now of standard BR (LMR) design. In April 1987 Class 20s Nos. 20128 and 20032 head a rake of MGR 'empties' onto the main line. Note the milepost on the right, proclaiming that the junction is 156½ miles from Paddington. *GD.*

LAWLEY BANK: The line from Ketley Junction (near Wellington) to Lightmoor was important to the GWR as not only did it provide a through route for passenger trains from Wellington to Buildwas Junction and Much Wenlock, but it also generated profitable goods traffic particularly from the Horsehay Iron Works. Lawley Bank was one of several Halts on the line catering for intermediate passenger traffic, featuring a shelter and crossing cabin. Above: It was a classic country railway scene in May 1955 as GWR 0—6—0PT No. 9741 called with the 12.48pm (SO) Ketley Town — Much Wenlock 'mixed'. The passenger service was withdrawn in 1962, and the branch from Ketley to Horsehay closed completely in 1964. A spur from Lightmoor to Horsehay was retained for access to the ironworks, but this too closed in 1981. *Geoff Bannister.*

Right: The neat little halt has been completely swept away, and in April 1987 the railway route was barely discernible; even the overhead cables and their posts have been moved as a result of road deviations. *JW.*

COALPORT (Shropshire) once boasted two stations, which although only a short distance apart were on opposite banks of the River Severn. On the west bank was the GWR station, serving the Shrewsbury — Bewdley Severn Valley line, while East station was at the end of the LNWR branch from Hadley. This had been promoted more with goods traffic in mind than passengers, although the service continued until 1952. Complete closure was in 1960. On January 3 1958 (below) Coalport East was a desolate sight, the station having fallen into disrepair; '9400' Class 0—6—0PT with a damaged smokebox number plate is shunting the goods yard. *Geoff Bannister.*

Below: On April 14 1987, the road bridge is still present, complete with cracks in the brick of the left-hand abutment. The station buildings have totally disappeared under a landscaped embankment and the roadway passes through what was once the goods yard. *GD.*

DONNINGTON: Close scrutiny of the right hand side of both views reveals a high wire fence, bordering the Ministry of Defence establishment at Donnington (Shropshire). The truncated remains of the Wellington — Stafford line still runs into the western end of this base, whilst the trackbed beyond has now been converted into the main A518 road from Wellington to Stafford. Above: Fowler 2—6—4T No. 42350 is pictured arriving at Donnington with a Stafford-bound stopping train, on June 12 1964, viewed from the signalbox. As pictured on April 14 1987, on this site today stands a traffic island, the centrepiece of which is an impressive clock tower donated by a local company.
Peter Shoesmith/JW.

NEWPORT (SALOP): Looking at this site today (left) it is difficult to believe that a railway ever existed here for the former up side is now a housing estate, whose gardens extend over the trackbed to the site of the down platform. The edging slabs still exist next to the mesh fence. A low embankment now carries the main road, for the bridge has been demolished. It is only on the left that the railway past survives, in the shape of the station house, still happily occupied in late 1987 by the family of the late station master. *GD.*

Below: A very different scene on June 12 1964, as Stanier Class 5MT 4—6—0 No. 45283 rolls to a halt with a three-coach Wellington — Stafford 'stopping' train comprised of LMS stock. Then, the station house was hidden behind the water tower, with only the near corner of the roof visible. The station closed in 1964, when the passenger service was withdrawn; complete closure followed in 1969. *Peter Shoesmith.*

GNOSALL on the Wellington — Stafford line is a quiet Staffordshire village which enjoyed a train service until 1964. Its station, situated on an embankment, had attractive wooden buildings with unusual barrel-shaped roofs. It was, without doubt, a charming place as the 'past' view (above) clearly shows, with BR Standard Class 5MT No. 73090 drawing to a halt with a Stafford — Wellington train. Beyond the train, at carriage window height is a dark triangle which is an abutment to a farm bridge. This becomes more evident (behind the walkers) in the 1987 view, for no other trace of the railway or station remains. *Peter Shoesmith/ GD.*